KT-371-655

Vegetarian

Everyday recipes to enjoy

vegetable soup with pesto

ingredients

SERVES 4

1 litre/1¾ pints fresh cold water
bouquet garni of 1 fresh parsley sprig, 1 fresh thyme sprig, and 1 bay leaf, tied together with clean string
2 celery stalks, chopped
3 baby leeks, chopped
4 baby carrots, chopped
150 g/5½ oz new potatoes, scrubbed and cut into bite-size chunks
4 tbsp shelled broad beans or peas
175 g/6 oz canned cannellini or flageolet beans, drained and rinsed
3 heads pak choi
150 g/5½ oz rocket
pepper

pesto

2 large handfuls fresh basil leaves
1 fresh green chilli, deseeded
2 garlic cloves
4 tbsp olive oil
1 tsp Parmesan-style vegetarian cheese

method

1 Put the water and bouquet garni into a large saucepan and add the celery, leeks, carrots and potatoes. Bring to the boil, then reduce the heat and simmer for 10 minutes.

2 Stir in the broad beans or peas and canned beans and simmer for a further 10 minutes. Stir in the pak choi and rocket, season with pepper and simmer for a further 2–3 minutes. Remove and discard the bouquet garni.

3 Meanwhile, to make the pesto, put the basil, chilli, garlic and oil into a food processor and pulse to form a thick paste. Stir in the cheese.

4 Stir most of the pesto into the soup, then ladle into warmed bowls. Top with the remaining pesto and serve at once.

greek salad

ingredients

SERVES 4

4 tomatoes, cut into wedges
1 onion, sliced
1/2 cucumber, sliced
225 g/8 oz kalamata olives, stoned
225 g/8 oz feta cheese, cubed
2 tbsp fresh coriander leaves
fresh flat-leaf parsley sprigs, to garnish
pitta bread, to serve

dressing

5 tbsp extra virgin olive oil
2 tbsp white wine vinegar
1 tbsp lemon juice
1/2 tsp sugar
1 tbsp chopped fresh coriander
salt and pepper

method

1 To make the dressing, put all the ingredients for the dressing into a large bowl and mix well together.

2 Add the tomatoes, onion, cucumber, olives, cheese and coriander. Toss all the ingredients together, then divide between individual serving bowls. Garnish with parsley sprigs and serve with pitta bread.

pasta salad with chargrilled peppers

ingredients

SERVES 4

1 red pepper
1 orange pepper
280 g/10 oz dried conchiglie
5 tbsp extra virgin olive oil
2 tbsp lemon juice
2 tbsp pesto
1 garlic clove
3 tbsp shredded fresh basil leaves
salt and pepper

method

1 Put the whole peppers on a baking sheet and place under a preheated grill, turning frequently, for 15 minutes, until charred all over. Remove with tongs and place in a bowl. Cover with crumpled kitchen paper and set aside.

2 Meanwhile, bring a large saucepan of lightly salted water to the boil. Add the pasta, bring back to the boil and cook for 8–10 minutes, until tender, but still firm to the bite.

3 Combine the olive oil, lemon juice, pesto and garlic in a bowl, whisking well to mix. Drain the pasta, add it to the pesto mixture while still hot and toss well. Set aside.

4 When the peppers are cool enough to handle, peel off the skins, then cut open and remove the seeds. Chop the flesh coarsely and add to the pasta with the basil. Season to taste with salt and pepper and toss well. Serve at room temperature.

warm red lentil salad with goat's cheese

ingredients

SERVES 4

2 tbsp olive oil
2 tsp cumin seeds
2 garlic cloves, crushed
2 tsp grated fresh ginger
300 g/10½ oz split red lentils
700 ml/1¼ pints vegetable stock
2 tbsp chopped fresh mint
2 tbsp chopped fresh coriander
2 red onions, thinly sliced
200 g/7 oz baby spinach leaves
1 tsp hazelnut oil
150 g/5½ oz soft goat's cheese
4 tbsp Greek-style yogurt
pepper
1 lemon, cut into quarters, to garnish
toasted rye bread, to serve

method

1 Heat half the olive oil in a large saucepan over medium heat, add the cumin seeds, garlic and ginger and cook for 2 minutes, stirring constantly.

2 Stir in the lentils, then add the stock, a ladleful at a time, until it is all absorbed, stirring constantly – this will take about 20 minutes. Remove from the heat and stir in the herbs.

3 Meanwhile, heat the remaining olive oil in a frying pan over medium heat, add the onions and cook, stirring frequently, for 10 minutes, or until soft and lightly browned.

4 Toss the spinach in the hazelnut oil in a bowl, then divide between 4 serving plates.

5 Mash the goat's cheese with the yogurt in a small bowl and season with pepper.

6 Divide the lentils between the serving plates and top with the onions and goat's cheese mixture. Garnish with lemon quarters and serve with toasted rye bread.

courgette fritters with yogurt dip

ingredients

SERVES 4

2–3 courgettes, about 400 g/14 oz
1 garlic clove, crushed
3 spring onions, finely sliced
125 g/4½ oz feta cheese, crumbled
2 tbsp finely chopped fresh parsley
2 tbsp finely chopped fresh mint
1 tbsp finely chopped fresh dill
½ tsp freshly grated nutmeg
2 tbsp all-purpose flour
pepper
2 eggs
2 tbsp olive oil
1 lemon, cut into quarters, to garnish

yogurt dip

250 g/9 oz strained plain yogurt
¼ cucumber, diced
1 tbsp finely chopped fresh dill
pepper

method

1 Grate the courgettes straight onto a clean tea towel and cover with another. Pat well and set aside for 10 minutes until the courgettes are dry.

2 Meanwhile, to make the dip, mix the yogurt, cucumber, dill and pepper in a serving bowl. Cover and chill.

3 Tip the courgettes into a large mixing bowl. Stir in the garlic, spring onions, cheese, herbs, nutmeg, flour and pepper. Beat the eggs in a separate bowl and stir into the courgette mixture – the batter will be quite lumpy and uneven but this is fine.

4 Heat the oil in a large, wide frying pan over medium heat. Drop 4 tablespoonfuls of the batter into the pan, with space in between, and cook for 2–3 minutes on each side. Remove, drain on kitchen paper and keep warm. Cook the second batch of fritters in the same way. (There should be 8 fritters in total.)

5 Serve the fritters hot with the dip, garnished with lemon quarters.

stuffed portobello mushrooms

ingredients

SERVES 4

12 large portobello mushrooms, wiped over and stems removed
2 tbsp sunflower oil, plus extra for oiling
1 fennel bulb, stalks removed, finely chopped
100 g/3½ oz sun-dried tomatoes, finely chopped
2 garlic cloves, crushed
125 g/4½ oz grated fontina cheese
50 g/1¾ oz freshly grated Parmesan-style vegetarian cheese
3 tbsp chopped fresh basil
salt and pepper
1 tbsp olive oil
fresh Parmesan-style vegetarian cheese shavings and chopped fresh parsley, to serve

method

1 Place 8 of the mushrooms, cup-side up, in a large, lightly oiled ovenproof dish and chop the remaining 4 mushrooms finely.

2 Heat the sunflower oil in a non-stick frying pan, add the chopped mushrooms, fennel, sun-dried tomatoes and garlic and cook over low heat until the vegetables are soft, but not browned. Remove from the heat and let cool.

3 When cool, add the cheeses, basil, salt and pepper. Mix well. Brush the mushrooms lightly with the olive oil and fill each cavity with a spoonful of the vegetable filling. Bake in a preheated oven, 180°C/350°F/Gas Mark 4, for 20–25 minutes, or until the mushrooms are tender and the filling is heated through.

4 Top with Parmesan-style cheese shavings and parsley and serve at once, allowing 2 mushrooms for each person.

stuffed red peppers with basil

ingredients

SERVES 4

140 g/5 oz long-grain white or brown rice
4 large red peppers
2 tbsp olive oil
1 garlic clove, chopped
4 shallots, chopped
1 celery stalk, chopped
3 tbsp chopped toasted walnuts
2 tomatoes, peeled and chopped
1 tbsp lemon juice
50 g/1¾ oz raisins
4 tbsp freshly grated Cheddar cheese
2 tbsp chopped fresh basil
salt and pepper
fresh basil sprigs, to garnish
lemon wedges, to serve

method

1 Cook the rice in a pan of lightly salted boiling water for 20 minutes, if using white rice, or 35 minutes, if using brown. Drain, rinse under cold running water, then drain again.

2 Using a sharp knife, cut the tops off the peppers and set aside. Remove the seeds and white cores, then blanch the peppers and reserved tops in boiling water for 2 minutes. Remove from the heat and drain well. Heat half the oil in a large frying pan. Add the garlic and shallots and cook, stirring, for 3 minutes. Add the celery, walnuts, tomatoes, lemon juice and raisins and cook for a further 5 minutes. Remove from the heat and stir in the rice, cheese, chopped basil, salt and pepper.

3 Stuff the peppers with the rice mixture and arrange them in a baking dish. Place the tops on the peppers, drizzle over the remaining oil, loosely cover with foil, and bake in a preheated oven, 180°C/350°F/Gas Mark 4, for 45 minutes. Remove from the oven, garnish with basil sprigs and serve with lemon wedges.

falafel with tahini sauce

ingredients

SERVES 4

450 g/1 lb canned cannellini beans, drained
350 g/12 oz canned chickpeas, drained
1 onion, finely chopped
2 garlic cloves, chopped
1 small fresh red chilli, deseeded and chopped
1 tsp baking powder
25 g/1 oz fresh parsley, chopped, plus extra sprigs to garnish
pinch of cayenne pepper
2 tbsp water
salt and pepper
vegetable oil, for deep-frying
pitta bread and lemon wedges, to serve

tahini sauce

200 ml/7 fl oz tahini
1 garlic clove, chopped
1–2 tbsp water
2–3 tsp lemon juice, to taste

method

1 To make the tahini sauce, put the tahini and garlic in a bowl. Gradually stir in the water until a fairly smooth consistency is reached, then stir in the lemon juice. Add more water or lemon juice, if necessary. Cover with clingfilm and chill in the refrigerator until required.

2 To make the falafel, rinse and drain the beans and chickpeas. Put them in a food processor with the onion, garlic, chilli, baking powder, chopped parsley and cayenne pepper. Process to a coarse paste, then add the water and season with plenty of salt and pepper. Process again briefly.

3 Heat about 6 cm/2½ inches of oil in a deep-fat fryer, large, heavy-based saucepan or wok over high heat. Deep-fry rounded tablespoonfuls of the mixture in batches for 2–2½ minutes until golden and crispy on the outside. Remove with a slotted spoon and drain well on kitchen paper. Serve hot or cold, garnished with parsley sprigs and accompanied by the tahini sauce, pitta bread and lemon wedges.

mexican three-bean chilli stew

ingredients

SERVES 6

140 g/5 oz each dried black beans, cannellini beans and borlotti beans, soaked overnight in separate bowls in water to cover
2 tbsp olive oil
1 large onion, finely chopped
2 red peppers, deseeded and diced
2 garlic cloves, very finely chopped
1/2 tsp cumin seeds, crushed
1 tsp coriander seeds, crushed
1 tsp dried oregano
1/2–2 tsp chilli powder
3 tbsp tomato purée
800 g/1 lb 12 oz canned chopped tomatoes
1 tsp sugar
1 tsp salt
600 ml/1 pint vegetable stock
3 tbsp chopped fresh coriander
slices of red onion and small pieces of avocado, to garnish

method

1 Drain the beans, put in separate saucepans and cover with cold water. Bring to the boil and boil vigorously for 10–15 minutes, then reduce the heat and simmer for 35–45 minutes until just tender. Drain and set aside.

2 Heat the oil in a large, heavy-based saucepan over medium heat. Add the onion and peppers and cook, stirring frequently, for 5 minutes, or until softened.

3 Add the garlic, cumin and coriander seeds and oregano and cook, stirring, for 30 seconds until the garlic is beginning to colour. Add the chilli powder and tomato purée and cook, stirring, for 1 minute. Add the tomatoes, sugar, salt, beans and stock. Bring to the boil, then reduce the heat, cover and simmer, stirring occasionally, for 45 minutes.

4 Stir in the fresh coriander. Ladle into individual warmed bowls and serve at once. Garnish with slices of red onion and small pieces of avocado.

roasted ratatouille & potato wedges

ingredients

SERVES 4

300 g/10½ oz potatoes in their skins, scrubbed
200 g/7 oz aubergine, cut into ½-inch/1-cm wedges
125 g/4½ oz red onion, cut into 5-mm/¼-inch slices
200 g/7 oz deseeded mixed peppers, sliced into 1-cm/½-inch strips
175 g/6 oz courgettes, cut in half lengthwise, then into 1-cm/½-inch slices
125 g/4½ oz cherry tomatoes
90 g/3¼ oz low-fat cream cheese
1 tsp runny honey
pinch of smoked paprika
1 tsp chopped fresh parsley

marinade

1 tsp fresh rosemary
1 tbsp fresh lemon thyme
1 tsp vegetable oil
1 tbsp lemon juice
4 tbsp white wine
1 tsp sugar
2 tbsp chopped fresh basil
½ tsp smoked paprika

method

1 Bake the potatoes in a preheated oven, 200°C/400°F/Gas Mark 6, for 30 minutes, then remove and cut into wedges – the flesh should not be completely cooked.

2 To make the marinade, finely chop the rosemary and lemon thyme, then place all the ingredients in a bowl and blend with a hand-held electric blender until smooth, or use a food processor.

3 Put the potato wedges into a large bowl with the aubergine, onion, peppers and courgettes, then pour over the marinade and mix thoroughly.

4 Arrange the vegetables on a non-stick baking sheet and roast in the oven, turning occasionally, for 25–30 minutes, or until golden brown and tender. Add the tomatoes for the last 5 minutes of the cooking time, just to split the skins and warm slightly.

5 Mix the cream cheese, honey and paprika together in a bowl.

6 Serve the vegetables with the cream cheese mixture and sprinkle with chopped parsley.

vegetarian lasagne

ingredients

SERVES 4

olive oil, for brushing
2 aubergines, sliced
2 tbsp butter
1 garlic clove, finely chopped
4 courgettes, sliced
1 tbsp finely chopped fresh flat-leaf parsley
1 tbsp finely chopped fresh marjoram
225 g/8 oz mozzarella cheese, grated
600 ml/1 pint strained canned tomatoes
175 g/6 oz dried no-precook lasagne sheets
salt and pepper
55 g/2 oz freshly grated Parmesan-style vegetarian cheese

béchamel sauce

300 ml/10 fl oz milk
1 bay leaf
6 black peppercorns
slice of onion
mace blade
2 tbsp butter
3 tbsp plain flour
salt and pepper

method

1 To make the béchamel sauce, pour the milk into a saucepan. Add the bay leaf, peppercorns, onion and mace. Heat to just below boiling point, then remove from the heat, cover, infuse for 10 minutes, then strain. Melt the butter in a separate saucepan. Sprinkle in the flour and cook over low heat, stirring constantly, for 1 minute. Gradually stir in the milk, then bring to the boil and cook, stirring, until thickened and smooth. Season with salt and pepper.

2 Brush a grill pan with olive oil and heat until smoking. Add half the aubergine slices and cook over medium heat for 8 minutes, or until golden brown all over. Remove from the grill pan and drain on kitchen paper. Repeat with the remaining aubergine slices.

3 Melt the butter in a frying pan and add the garlic, courgettes, parsley and marjoram. Cook over medium heat, stirring frequently, for 5 minutes, or until the courgettes are golden all over. Remove and drain on kitchen paper.

4 Layer the aubergine, courgettes, mozzarella, tomatoes and lasagne sheets in an ovenproof dish brushed with olive oil, seasoning as you go and finishing with a layer of lasagne. Pour over the béchamel sauce, making sure that all the pasta is covered. Sprinkle with Parmesan-style cheese and bake in a preheated oven, 200°C/ 400°F/Gas Mark 6, for 30–40 minutes, or until golden brown. Serve at once.

creamy spinach & mushroom pasta

ingredients

SERVES 4

300 g/10½ oz dried penne or pasta of your choice

2 tbsp olive oil

250 g/9 oz mushrooms, sliced

1 tsp dried oregano

275 ml/9 fl oz vegetable stock

1 tbsp lemon juice

6 tbsp cream cheese

200 g/7 oz frozen spinach leaves

salt and pepper

method

1 Cook the pasta in a large pan of lightly salted boiling water, according to the packet instructions. Drain, reserving 175 ml/6 fl oz of the cooking liquid.

2 Meanwhile, heat the oil in a large, heavy-based frying pan over medium heat, add the mushrooms and cook, stirring frequently, for 8 minutes, or until almost crisp. Stir in the oregano, stock and lemon juice and cook for 10–12 minutes, or until the sauce is reduced by half.

3 Stir in the cream cheese and spinach and cook over medium–low heat for 3–5 minutes. Add the reserved cooking liquid, then the cooked pasta. Stir well, season to taste with salt and pepper and heat through gently before serving.

chinese vegetables & beansprouts with noodles

ingredients

SERVES 4

1.2 litres/2 pints vegetable stock
1 garlic clove, crushed
1-cm/1/2-inch piece fresh ginger, finely chopped
225 g/8 oz dried medium egg noodles
1 red pepper, deseeded and sliced
85 g/3 oz frozen peas
115 g/4 oz broccoli florets
85 g/3 oz shiitake mushrooms, sliced
2 tbsp sesame seeds
225 g/8 oz canned water chestnuts, drained and halved
225 g/8 oz canned bamboo shoots, drained
280 g/10 oz Napa cabbage, sliced
140 g/5 oz beansprouts
3 spring onions, sliced
1 tbsp dark soy sauce
pepper

method

1 Bring the stock, garlic and ginger to the boil in a large saucepan. Stir in the noodles, red pepper, peas, broccoli and mushrooms and return to the boil. Reduce the heat, cover, and simmer for 5–6 minutes, or until the noodles are tender.

2 Meanwhile, preheat the grill to medium. Spread the sesame seeds out in a single layer on a baking sheet and toast under the preheated grill, turning to brown evenly – watch constantly because they brown very quickly. Tip the sesame seeds into a small dish and set aside.

3 Once the noodles are tender, add the water chestnuts, bamboo shoots, Napa cabbage, beansprouts and spring onions to the pan. Return the stock to the boil, stir to mix the ingredients and simmer for a further 2–3 minutes to heat through thoroughly.

4 Carefully drain off 300 ml/10 fl oz of the stock into a small heatproof jug and set aside. Drain and discard any remaining stock and turn the noodles and vegetables into a warmed serving dish. Quickly mix the soy sauce with the reserved stock and pour over the noodles and vegetables. Season with pepper and serve at once.

vegetarian paella

ingredients

SERVES 4

1/2 tsp saffron threads
2 tbsp hot water
6 tbsp olive oil
1 Spanish onion, sliced
3 garlic cloves, minced
1 red pepper, deseeded and sliced
1 orange pepper, deseeded and sliced
1 large aubergine, cubed
200 g/7 oz medium-grain paella rice
600 ml/1 pint vegetable stock
450 g/1 lb tomatoes, peeled and chopped
salt and pepper
115 g/4 oz mushrooms, sliced
115 g/4 oz green beans, halved
400 g/14 oz canned borlotti beans

method

1 Put the saffron threads and water in a small bowl or cup and infuse for a few minutes.

2 Meanwhile, heat the oil in a paella pan or wide, shallow frying pan and cook the onion over medium heat, stirring, for 2–3 minutes, or until softened. Add the garlic, peppers and aubergine and cook, stirring frequently, for 5 minutes.

3 Add the rice and cook, stirring constantly, for 1 minute, or until glossy and coated. Pour in the stock and add the tomatoes, saffron and its soaking water, salt and pepper. Bring to the boil, then reduce the heat and simmer, shaking the pan frequently and stirring occasionally, for 15 minutes.

4 Stir in the mushrooms, green beans and borlotti beans with their can juices. Cook for a further 10 minutes, then serve immediately.

risotto primavera

ingredients

SERVES 6–8

225 g/8 oz fresh thin asparagus spears
4 tbsp olive oil
175 g/6 oz young green beans, cut into 2.5-cm/1-inch lengths
175 g/6 oz young courgettes, quartered and cut into 2.5-cm/1-inch lengths
225 g/8 oz shelled fresh peas
1 onion, finely chopped
1–2 garlic cloves, finely chopped
350 g/12 oz Arborio rice
1.5 litres/2¾ pints simmering vegetable stock
4 spring onions, cut into 2.5-cm/1-inch lengths
salt and pepper
55 g/2 oz butter
115 g/4 oz freshly grated Parmesan-style vegetarian cheese
2 tbsp snipped fresh chives
2 tbsp shredded fresh basil
spring onions, to garnish (optional)

method

1 Trim the woody ends of the asparagus and cut off the tips. Cut the stems into 2.5-cm/1-inch pieces and set aside with the tips.

2 Heat 2 tablespoons of the oil in a large frying pan over high heat until very hot. Add the asparagus, beans, courgettes and peas and stir-fry for 3–4 minutes until they are bright green and just starting to soften. Set aside.

3 Heat the remaining oil in a large, heavy-based pan over medium heat. Add the onion and cook, stirring occasionally, for 3 minutes, or until it starts to soften. Stir in the garlic and cook, while stirring, for 30 seconds. Reduce the heat, add the rice and mix to coat in oil. Cook, stirring constantly, for 2–3 minutes, or until the grains are translucent.

4 Gradually add the hot stock, a ladleful at a time. Stir constantly and add more liquid as the rice absorbs each addition. Increase the heat to medium so that the liquid bubbles. Cook for 20 minutes, or until all but 2 tablespoons of the liquid is absorbed and the rice is creamy.

5 Stir in the stir-fried vegetables, onion mixture and spring onions with the remaining stock. Cook for 2 minutes, stirring frequently, then season with salt and pepper. Stir in the butter, Parmesan-style cheese, chives and basil. Remove the pan from the heat and serve the risotto at once, garnished with spring onions, if liked.

This edition published by Parragon Books Ltd in 2013
LOVE FOOD is an imprint of Parragon Books Ltd

Parragon Books Ltd
Chartist House
15–17 Trim Street
Bath BA1 1HA, UK
www.parragon.com/lovefood

ISBN 978-1-4723-2236-4

Printed in China

Notes for the Reader

This book uses both metric and imperial measurements. Follow the same units of measurement throughout; do not mix metric and imperial. All spoon measurements are level: teaspoons are assumed to be 5 ml, and tablespoons are assumed to be 15 ml. Unless otherwise stated, milk is assumed to be full fat, eggs and individual vegetables are medium, and pepper is freshly ground black pepper. Unless otherwise stated, all root vegetables should be washed in plain water and peeled prior to using.

Garnishes, decorations and serving suggestions are all optional and not necessarily included in the recipe ingredients or method.

The times given are an approximate guide only. Preparation times differ according to the techniques used by different people and the cooking times may also vary from those given. Optional ingredients, variations or serving suggestions have not been included in the time calculations.

Recipes using raw or very lightly cooked eggs should be avoided by infants, the elderly, pregnant women, convalescents and anyone suffering from an illness. Pregnant and breastfeeding women are advised to avoid eating peanuts and peanut products. Sufferers from nut allergies should be aware that some of the ready-made ingredients used in the recipes in this book may contain nuts. Always check the packaging before use.

Vegetarians should be aware that some of the ready-made ingredients used in the recipes in this book may contain animal products. Always check the packaging before use.